D1299125

ASK A
BUG

Olivia Brookes

PowerKiDS
press.

New York

Published in 2009 by The Rosen Publishing Group, Inc.
29 East 21st Street, New York, NY 10010

Created and produced by: Julia Bruce,
Rachel Coombs, Nicholas Harris, Sarah Hartley, and
Erica Simms, Orpheus Books Ltd

U.S. editor: Kara Murray

Illustrated by: Ian Jackson (*The Art Agency*)
Other illustrations by: Fiammetta Dogi,
Sauro Giampaia, and David Wright

Consultant: Darren J. Mann
The Oxford University Museum
of Natural History, England

Library of Congress Cataloging-in-Publication Data

Brookes, Olivia.
A bug / Olivia Brookes. — 1st ed.
p. cm. — (Ask)
Includes index.
ISBN 978-1-4358-2514-7 (library binding)
1. Insects—Juvenile literature. I. Title.
QL467.2.B76 2009
595.7—dc22
2008004525

Manufactured in China

contents

Introduction

We may be small, but we bugs lead lives full of danger and excitement. We are here to tell you a little about what it's like to be one of us. You'll find out how we catch our prey but avoid being eaten ourselves, how we find a mate and keep our eggs and young safe, and how we can survive at all in a world of giants. Our lives are full of wonders. Read on and you'll meet a swarm of locusts and the largest centipede in the world. You'll find out why a ladybug has spots, what goes on inside a termite mound, and how spiders make their webs. Come face to face with a praying mantis and have dinner with a mosquito and a bluebottle fly. But first of all, come and meet one of the most beautiful insects in the world, the blue morpho butterfly.

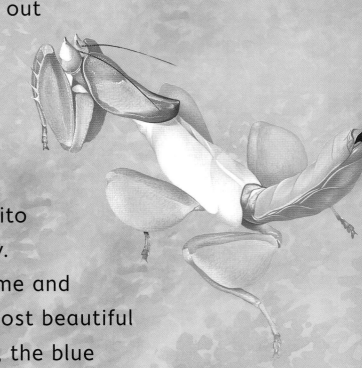

How Does a Caterpillar Become a Butterfly?

1 These green buttons are really eggs stuck to a leaf. One is mine. I will hatch in 9 or 10 days.

2 Now I'm a colorful caterpillar coming out of my egg. My bright colors warn that I could be poisonous.

3 I spend all my time eating.

4 As I grow, I get too large for my skin. When it gets too tight, my old skin splits and peels off. But underneath is a new one that fits much better.

5 I have eight pairs of legs. Each foot has tiny hooks to help me hold on to branches. I hold on so tightly that it's hard for birds and other predators to pull me off and eat me.

6 After 11 weeks, I've eaten enough food. Now I attach myself to a twig and become a chrysalis. This is the last stage in my life before I become an adult butterfly.

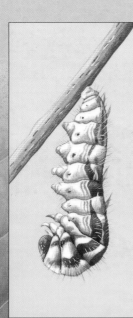

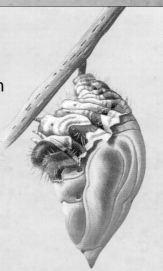

7 I spin a case around myself. So that I won't be noticed, it looks like a leaf. Inside, my body changes from a caterpillar to a butterfly.

8 After about two weeks, I pull my new self out of my case. I'm now a blue morpho butterfly! It takes a while for my wings to become strong enough for me to fly. I will live only for about two more weeks. During that time, I need to find both food and a mate.

9 To draw a mate to me, I show off my blue wings as I fly. The dull color underneath helps me hide.

Why Do Insects Use Camouflage?

To my enemies I look like a bee with a deadly stinger. This keeps me from being eaten. But I am really just a harmless drone fly.

Life can be dangerous for us insects—lots of animals and birds would love to eat us! So we use camouflage to hide ourselves among our surroundings. Some of us use our color to blend in with leaves and flowers. Others fool predators by looking like scarier insects.

I am a stick insect. I am the same color as the plants I hide among. My body also looks like a plant stem.

Young peppered moth caterpillars can hide, too. They look just like twigs.

Look very closely— can you see us? There are two peppered moths resting on this branch. We are perfectly hidden against patches of lichen that grow on tree bark. Some, like me, are a darker color. You could see me on pale lichen, but on the brown tree bark, I'm very hard to see.

I am a bush cricket. I live in the trees of the Amazon rain forest in South America. When I sit still, I look like a leaf so other animals can't see me. If they attack, the large, eye-shaped marks under my wings appear. These make me look bigger.

I am a grasshopper from South Africa. My bright colors make me stand out, but they also warn predators that I might spray them with a stinky green froth if they try to eat me. Watch out!

I am a Hercules moth caterpillar. I am huge—6 inches (15 cm) long—so I can't hide very easily. I'm not actually poisonous, but by showing off my bright colors, I fool predators into thinking I am.

How Does a Dragonfly capture Prey?

I am a dragonfly. I am a fierce hunter just like a dragon. My mom laid her eggs in this pond. When my brothers and sisters and I first hatch, we are called nymphs. We live in the water for up to two years. We prey on other insects, tadpoles, and small fish until we are big enough to hunt for ourselves.

1 This is me as a nymph. I catch my prey by hunting or just by sitting still on the bottom of the stream and waiting for prey to come by.

3 I am now ready to change into an adult dragonfly. I climb out of the water and attach myself to a plant's stem.

2 This is my head up close. A clawed mask covers my face. When prey comes near, I grab it with my claws and pull it into my mouth.

4 This is me pulling myself out of my old skin. My wings are all crumpled. It will take a while for them to flatten out. I am not very strong yet. This is a dangerous time in my life. I could be eaten by my enemies anytime.

5 I am now a fully grown-up dragonfly. I will soon fly away from the water and spend two or three weeks eating. I will return to the water and find a mate. We adults only stop flying when we sleep. Whew!

6 Now that I'm big, I don't need a clawed mask to catch my prey. Instead I grab flying insects with my front legs and pull them into my strong jaws.

HOW DO Flies Feed?

I am a bluebottle fly. I bet you've swatted lots of us from your food. We do carry lots of germs on our feet, but we also do good by eating up dead, rotten things.

I lay eggs on dead animals or plants. Garbage cans and dumps are great places to find these. I lay up to 100 eggs. They hatch into larvae (called maggots) after a few days. They eat all the time for a week. Then they turn into adult flies.

A female mosquito like me needs fresh blood for my eggs to grow. I find warm-blooded animals, like humans, and cut into their skin with my sharp needlelike mouth. I drink until I am full. I can carry a tiny parasite that goes into my victim's body. This causes an illness called malaria.

Hairs on my body tell me when I touch things. They also allow me to feel the smallest air movements.

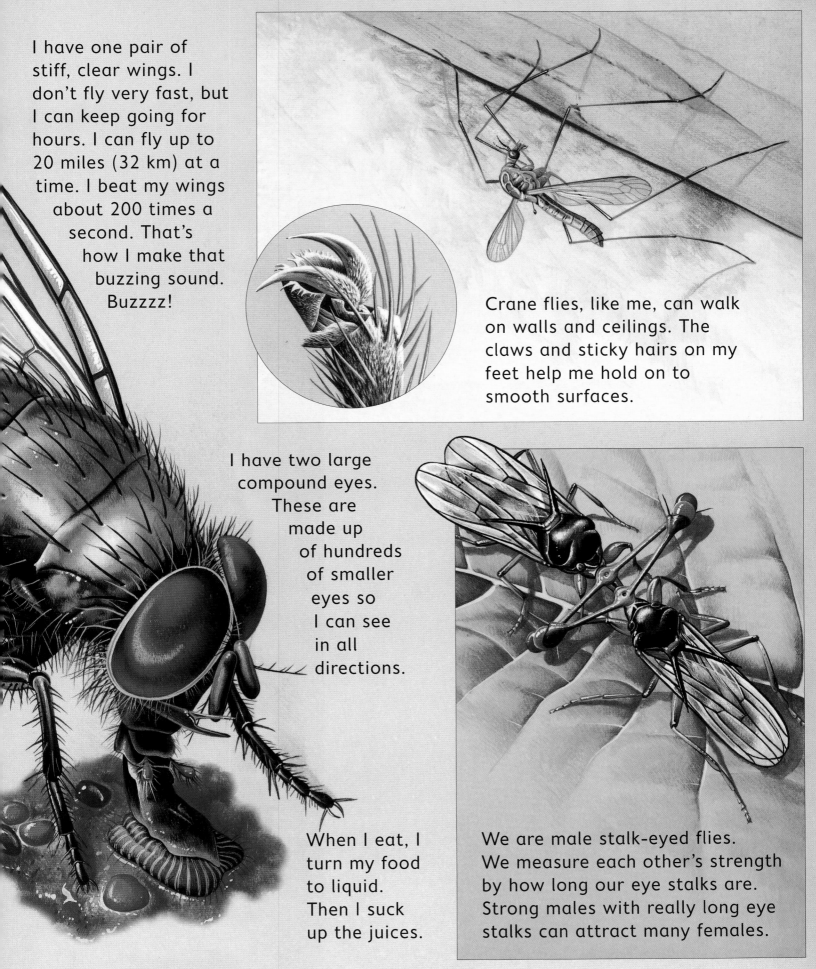

I have one pair of stiff, clear wings. I don't fly very fast, but I can keep going for hours. I can fly up to 20 miles (32 km) at a time. I beat my wings about 200 times a second. That's how I make that buzzing sound. Buzzzz!

Crane flies, like me, can walk on walls and ceilings. The claws and sticky hairs on my feet help me hold on to smooth surfaces.

I have two large compound eyes. These are made up of hundreds of smaller eyes so I can see in all directions.

When I eat, I turn my food to liquid. Then I suck up the juices.

We are male stalk-eyed flies. We measure each other's strength by how long our eye stalks are. Strong males with really long eye stalks can attract many females.

What's It Like to Be Queen Bee?

I am the queen bee in my hive. The two other kinds of honeybee are workers (other females) and drones (males).

Worker bees take care of me.

There are thousands of female worker bees. They feed larvae, collect nectar, and clean the hive.

1 I mate with a drone just once in my four-year life.

2 I lay eggs into cells that the workers have made out of wax.

3 Three days later my eggs hatch into larvae.

4 My workers spread my scent around the hive to stop other females from laying eggs.

5 After nine days, the larvae are closed inside the honeycomb. There they turn into worker bees.

6 When the bees come out, their bodies are soft.

7 This larva will become a new queen bee.

8 The hive has grown too big. I take a large group of workers and go to another tree to start a new colony.

HOW DO Different Ants Live?

I am a wood ant. We are very common in Europe and North America. I am one of the workers. I do many jobs for my colony. I clean the nest and collect food and water.

Did you know that there are likely more ants on Earth than any other insect? Ants live in groups called colonies. Large female queen ants lay all the eggs. The rest of us work to keep the colony running smoothly.

We are leafcutter ants. We can carry leaves that are much heavier than we are. We take these leaves back to our nest. There we chew them up so that a tasty fungus can grow on them.

We are weaver ants. You'll find us some places in Africa, Asia, and Australia. Here we are very busy tying leaves together to make a nest. Some of the queen's eggs have hatched into larvae. The larvae make the silk we need to tie the leaves together. We hold the larvae in our jaws and squeeze them to produce silk.

I am a honeypot ant. I live in hot, dry areas. During the rainy season, I store water in my tummy. When food is hard to find in the dry season, I feed the other ants in the colony.

I am a bulldog ant from Australia. I have long, spiky jaws. I use them to attack predators and for catching food.

We dairy ants are known for farming aphids. The aphids let us take their honeydew, a sweet liquid that is left over as waste when they eat leaves. We stroke them with our feelers to help them make this honeydew. In return, we keep the aphids safe from their predators, such as ladybugs.

Be warned, these jaws can give you a nasty bite!

Why Do Termites Live in Mounds?

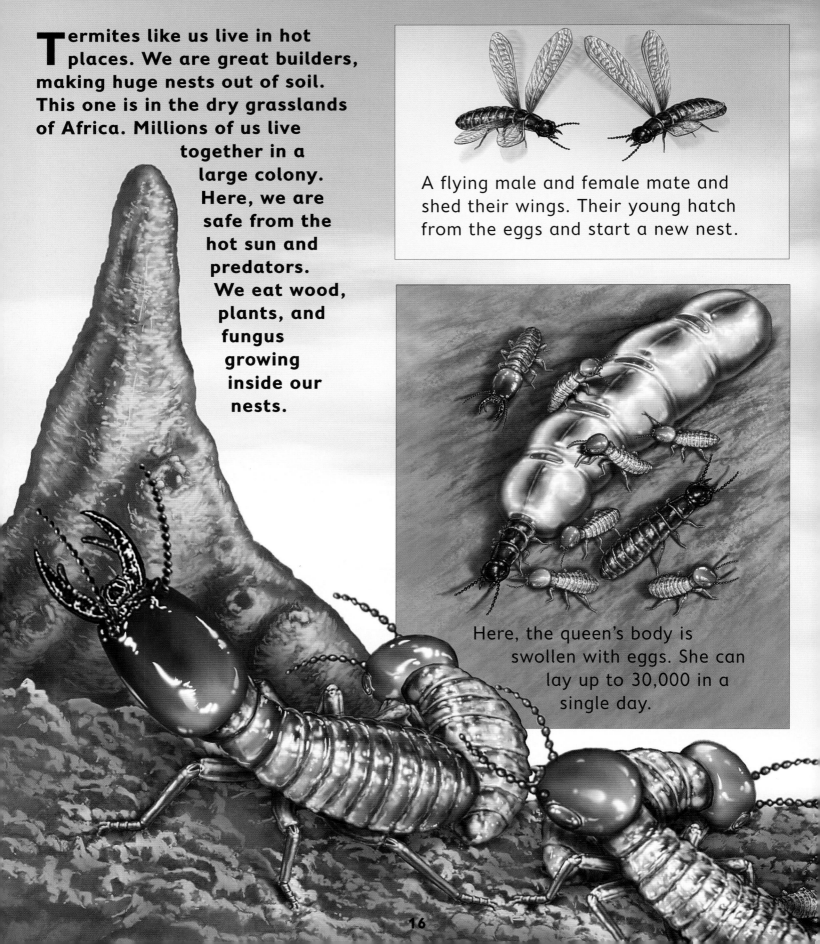

Termites like us live in hot places. We are great builders, making huge nests out of soil. This one is in the dry grasslands of Africa. Millions of us live together in a large colony. Here, we are safe from the hot sun and predators. We eat wood, plants, and fungus growing inside our nests.

A flying male and female mate and shed their wings. Their young hatch from the eggs and start a new nest.

Here, the queen's body is swollen with eggs. She can lay up to 30,000 in a single day.

Most soldier termites are blind. With those jaws, they can't even feed themselves.

Ants are our worst enemies. They search our nest for food and attack us when we are outside. Soldier termites keep the colony safe.

Our nest can measure up to 13 feet (4 m) high. This is what it looks like inside. The tunnels leading outside give us fresh air.

Most young termites are born without wings. Those who do have them will fly away and start a new nest.

Why Do Locusts Swarm?

We locusts are a type of grasshopper. We live in dry deserts and grasslands. Our dull colors help us hide safely in the grass. We grow to about 3 inches (8 cm) long and have strong back legs for jumping. When we are adults, we also have wings.

1 When it rains on our dry grassland, it is a good time for locusts to mate because there is plenty of food. In about two weeks, there are thousands of us. Unlike adults, the young born after the rains are very brightly colored. We don't need to use camouflage to stay safe because there are so many of us.

2 When we first hatch, we have no wings. We are called hoppers. We eat new shoots of grass that have grown fresh from the rainy season.

We locusts can travel up to 50 miles (80 km) in a day. But during the hottest part of the day, we rest in trees. We fly in search of new food in mornings and evenings when it's cooler.

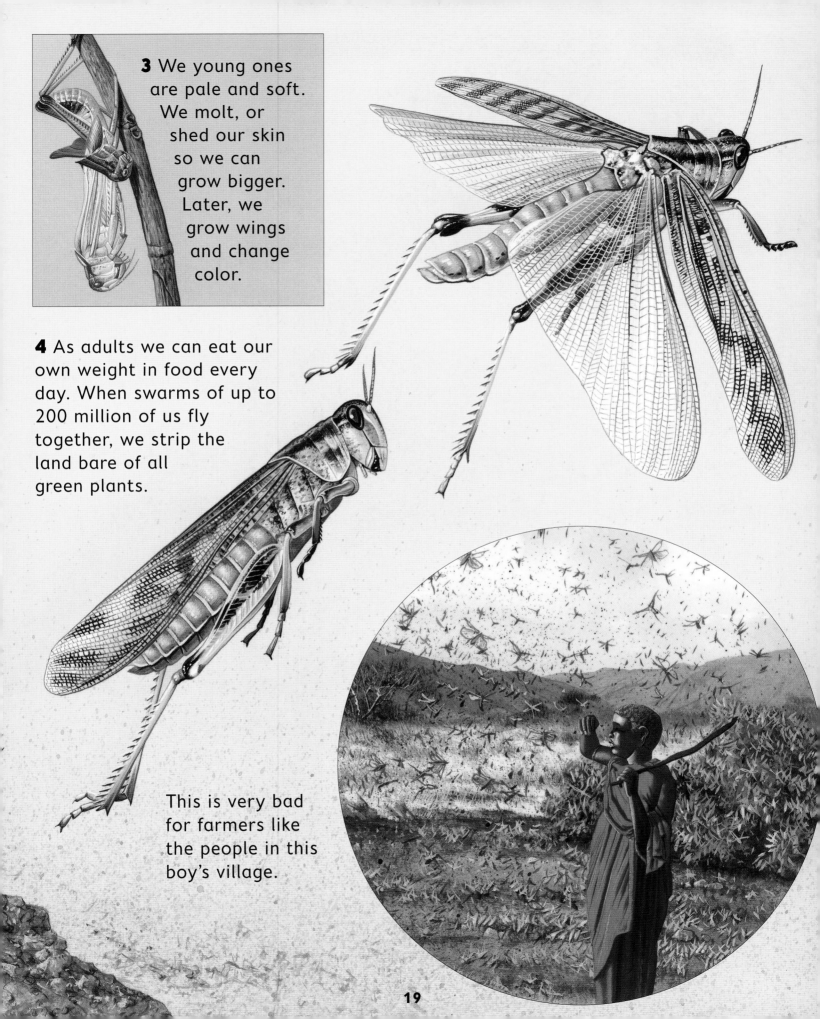

3 We young ones are pale and soft. We molt, or shed our skin so we can grow bigger. Later, we grow wings and change color.

4 As adults we can eat our own weight in food every day. When swarms of up to 200 million of us fly together, we strip the land bare of all green plants.

This is very bad for farmers like the people in this boy's village.

19

How Does a Praying Mantis Hunt?

I depend on my sharp eyesight to find my prey. I have compound eyes, like many other insects. They are so large that I can even see behind me. I can spot something good to eat moving up to 20 yards (18 m) away.

I am called a praying mantis because I hold my front legs together as if I were praying. Some of us chase after our prey, but most of us like to ambush them, or catch them by surprise. We stay so still that our prey don't know we are there—that is, until it's too late! We grab our victims with our front legs. We really like to eat flies and grasshoppers.

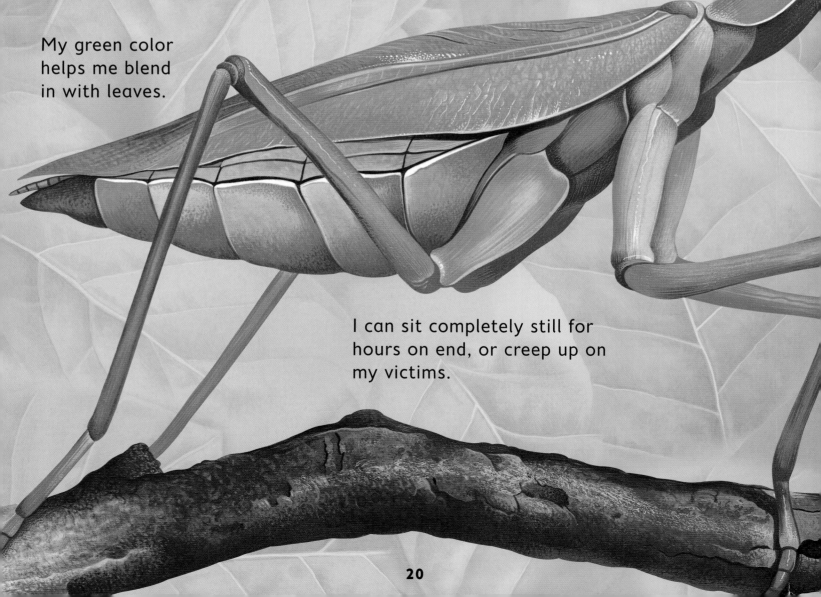

My green color helps me blend in with leaves.

I can sit completely still for hours on end, or creep up on my victims.

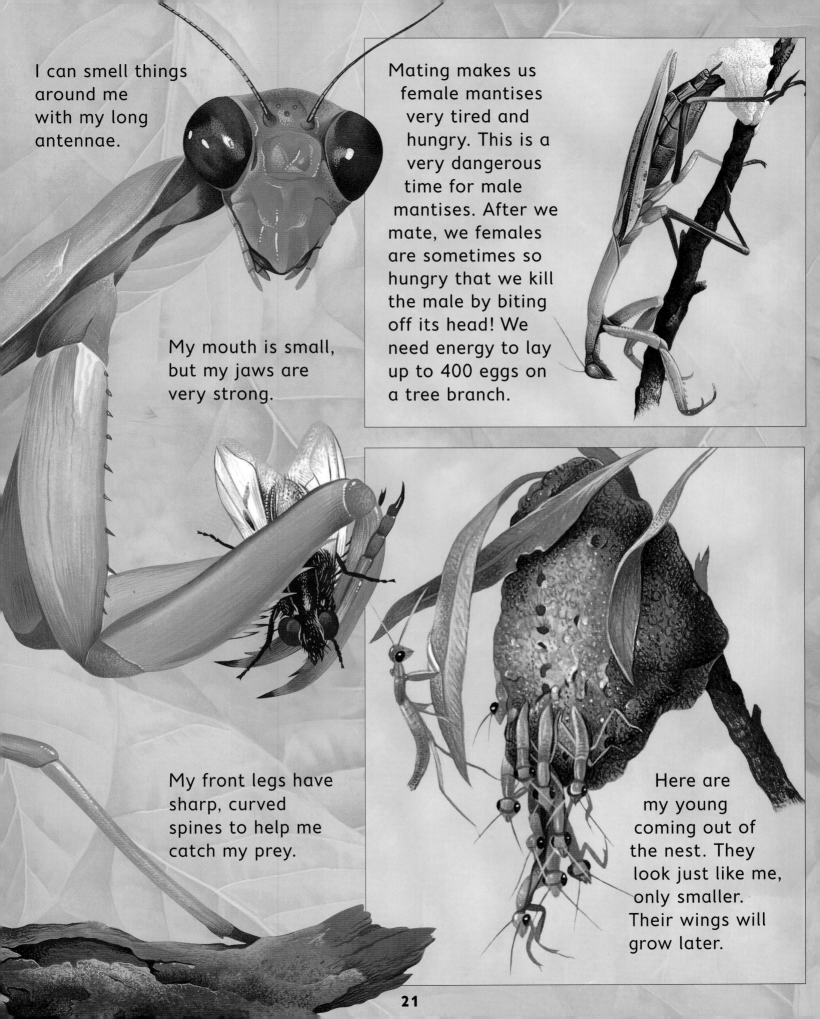

I can smell things around me with my long antennae.

My mouth is small, but my jaws are very strong.

My front legs have sharp, curved spines to help me catch my prey.

Mating makes us female mantises very tired and hungry. This is a very dangerous time for male mantises. After we mate, we females are sometimes so hungry that we kill the male by biting off its head! We need energy to lay up to 400 eggs on a tree branch.

Here are my young coming out of the nest. They look just like me, only smaller. Their wings will grow later.

HOW DO BEETLES LIVE?

Did you know there are more than 350,000 different types of beetle in the world? Nearly half of all insects are beetles, and we each have different ways of life.

I am a great diving beetle. I can fly, but I spend most of my time in streams, lakes and ponds, where I live under the water. I breathe by taking a bubble of air under my wing cases when I dive. I use my flat, hairy back legs like oars when I swim. I can swim very fast after my prey. I like to eat tadpoles, insect larvae and small fish.

Dung beetles like me live all over the world. We help clean up after animals like zebras and cows. Here I am rolling up a ball of elephant dung. When I'm done, I'll bury it and lay an egg there. My young will be safe inside when they hatch. They will grow up to eat dung, too.

I am a male stag beetle. We grow up to 3 inches (8 cm) long. Females are a little smaller. We only live for a few months, so finding a mate is the most important thing we do. Males like me fight with each other to win a female and guard our territory.

I am a tiger beetle. I can run faster than any other beetle.

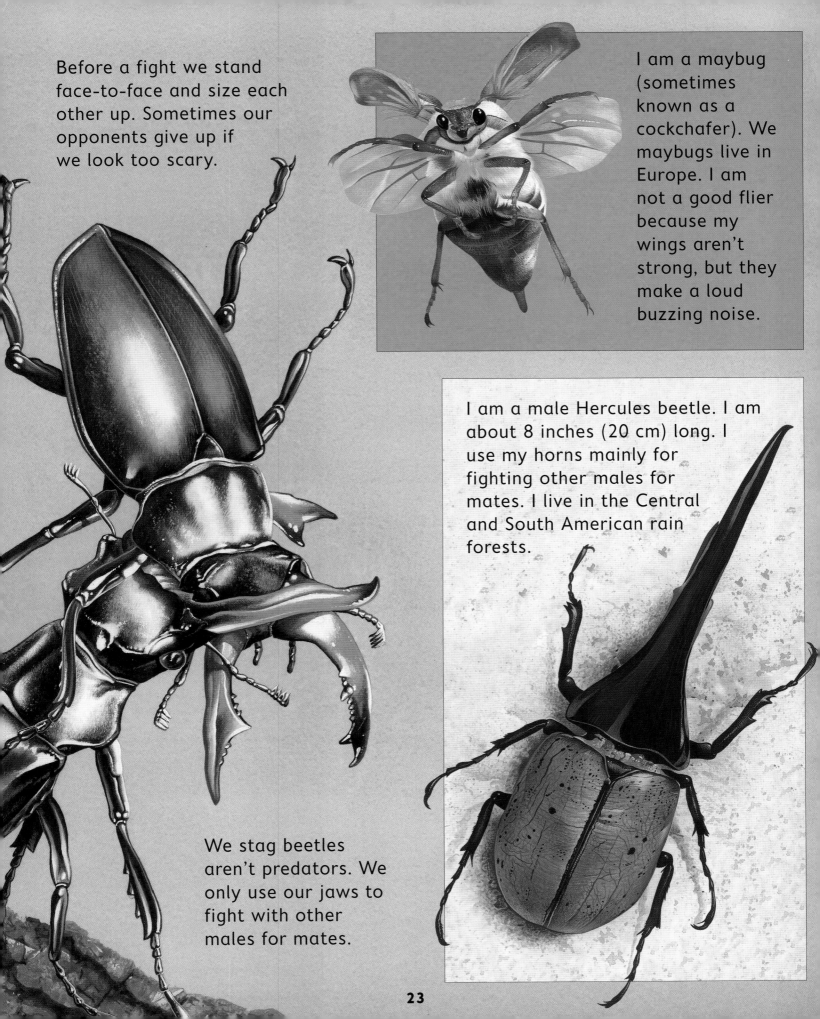

Before a fight we stand face-to-face and size each other up. Sometimes our opponents give up if we look too scary.

I am a maybug (sometimes known as a cockchafer). We maybugs live in Europe. I am not a good flier because my wings aren't strong, but they make a loud buzzing noise.

I am a male Hercules beetle. I am about 8 inches (20 cm) long. I use my horns mainly for fighting other males for mates. I live in the Central and South American rain forests.

We stag beetles aren't predators. We only use our jaws to fight with other males for mates.

Why Does a Ladybug Have Spots?

We ladybugs are really beetles. We are many different colors and often have spots. That's me, the seven-spot ladybug in the middle. There are nearly 6,000 other kinds. Our bright colors and marks show predators that we are not good to eat.

Aphids are our favorite food.

Hard cases keep our wings safe when we aren't flying. Like many other bugs, we can't fly when it's cold outside. We sleep in a group all winter until the days are warm again. This is called hibernation.

Ants try to keep aphids safe from us hungry ladybugs. We have to fight the ants so that we can feed aphids to our larvae when they hatch.

How Many Legs Does a Centipede Have?

All insects have six legs, but not all creepy crawlies are insects. We centipedes have at least 30 legs. Some of us even have 100 or more.

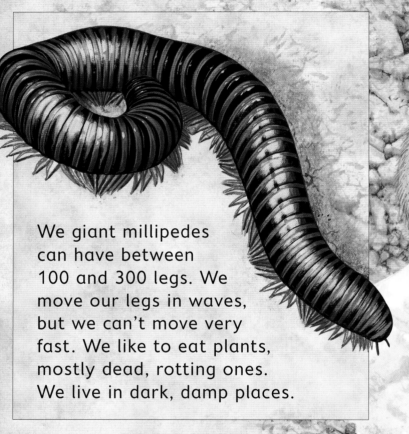

We giant millipedes can have between 100 and 300 legs. We move our legs in waves, but we can't move very fast. We like to eat plants, mostly dead, rotting ones. We live in dark, damp places.

I am a giant centipede. Growing up to 12 inches (30 cm) long, I am fast and fierce. I prey on snakes, frogs, and even small mammals.

When danger threatens, I curl up into a ball and tuck my legs in.

I am a red velvet mite. My color tells enemies to stay away. I am about the size of a pinhead. Like spiders and scorpions, I have eight legs. I live in soil and leaves in woodlands.

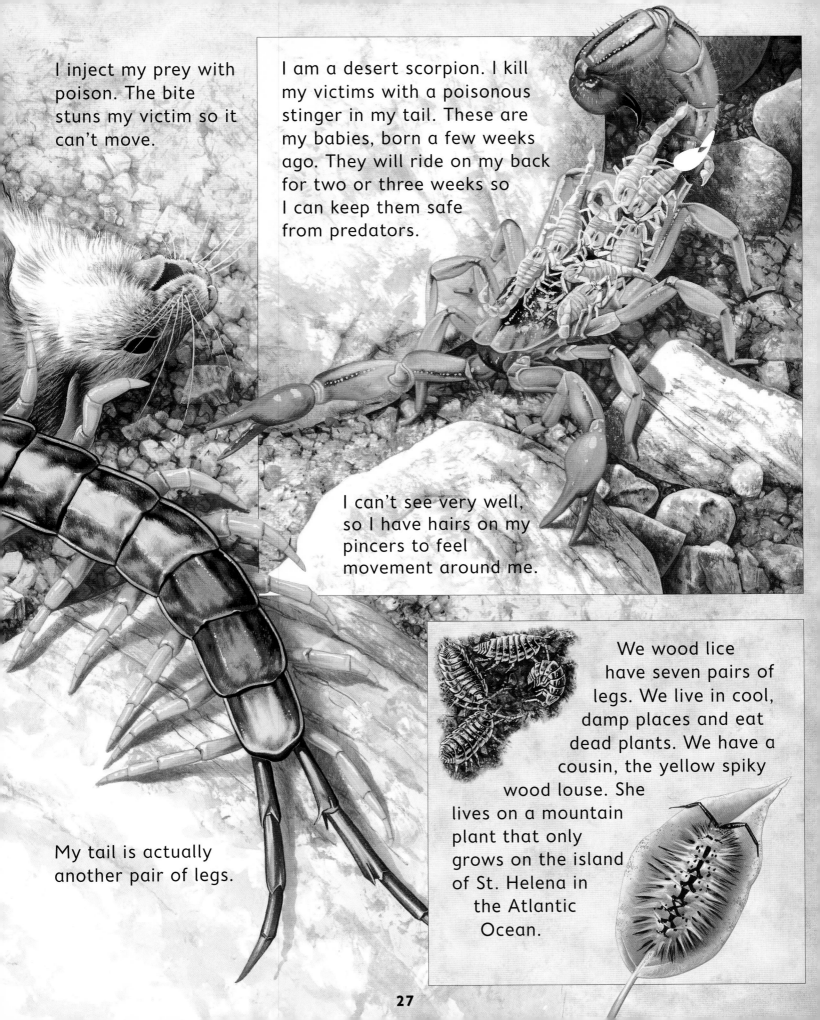

I inject my prey with poison. The bite stuns my victim so it can't move.

I am a desert scorpion. I kill my victims with a poisonous stinger in my tail. These are my babies, born a few weeks ago. They will ride on my back for two or three weeks so I can keep them safe from predators.

I can't see very well, so I have hairs on my pincers to feel movement around me.

My tail is actually another pair of legs.

We wood lice have seven pairs of legs. We live in cool, damp places and eat dead plants. We have a cousin, the yellow spiky wood louse. She lives on a mountain plant that only grows on the island of St. Helena in the Atlantic Ocean.

How Do Spiders Spin Their Webs?

We spiders are great spinners. I am an orb spider. I spin webs of sticky silk to catch my prey. Then I sit in the middle of my web and wait for my victims to land on it. I keep my feet on a thread called a signal line. This moves if anything lands on my web. I can even tell if it's real prey or just a leaf landing on my web. I also know which part of my web the victim has landed on. My webs usually only last for a day. When I lose one web, I just start again. I can make several webs in one day if I have to.

Once I catch something in my web, I wind it in silk so that it can't get away. I will come back later to eat it.

My web is so fine that it's very hard to see. Insects fly into it without knowing it's there. This is how I make a web. First I cast a long silk thread into the wind. Once it catches on a branch, I pull on it to make it tight. This is the hardest part.

1 I walk along the first thread and spin another.

2 I attach the second one to another branch.

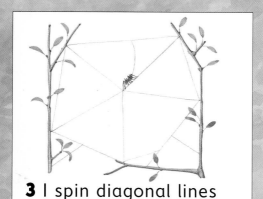

3 I spin diagonal lines that meet in the middle.

4 I weave a spiral of silk around and around.

5 Now I sit in the middle and wait for lunch!

All spiders can spin silk, but we don't all make webs. Silk comes from a liquid stored inside our bodies in organs called spinnerets.

I paralyze my prey with one bite. This stops the insect from struggling, but it doesn't kill it. A living insect will stay fresh so I can eat it later.

We ogre-faced spiders catch our prey using webs like nets. When a tasty-looking insect comes along, we drop the web down on top of it.

Do Spiders Hunt Birds?

We spiders use silk for many things besides making webs. It comes in handy for spinning a lifeline when we have to drop down from great heights. I use silk to make a protective case for my eggs before they hatch. And who am I? I am a Mexican red-kneed tarantula, one of the largest spiders in the world. I am at least as big as your hand.

I catch my prey by pouncing on them when they come close. Then I inject them with poison from my sharp fangs. This paralyzes them so they can't get away.

We trapdoor spiders catch prey by covering a small hole with a silk lid. We sit very still under it until it's time to pounce and drag it underground.

I have eight eyes, but my eyesight is not very good. I can only see light and dark and feel movement.

With the hair on my legs, I can feel the smallest movements on the ground and in the air.

We ogre-faced spiders have very good eyesight. I use my six eyes to catch prey both day and night.

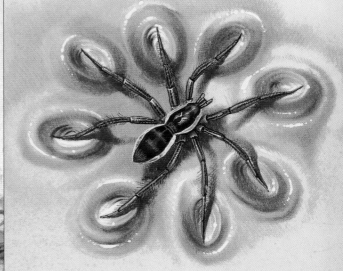

I am a fishing spider. I skate on the water looking for tadpoles and small fish. When my legs feel one, I dive down to catch it.

We are often called bird-eating spiders, but we do not often catch birds. We are more likely to eat frogs, small snakes, and larger insects. We even eat other spiders. This lizard will make a tasty meal.

Spitting spiders like me shoot poisoned silk at our prey. The bug gets all tangled up!

Glossary

antennae (an-TEH-nee) The special organs on an insect's head that can feel things around it.

camouflage (KA-muh-flahj) Colors and marks that help an animal or insect hide.

chrysalis (KRIH-suh-lus) The stage of a butterfly's life when it changes into its adult form.

compound eye (KOM-pownd EY) An eye with many lenses found in many insects.

fungus (FUN-gis) A living thing that is like a plant, but that does not have leaves, flowers, or green color, and that does not make its own food.

hatch (HACH) To come out of an egg.

insect (IN-sekt) An animal without a backbone whose body is divided into a head, thorax, and abdomen. Attached to the thorax are three pairs of legs.

larva (LAHR-vuh) The young of an insect that looks different from its adult form; for example, caterpillars.

molting (MOHLT-ing) The shedding of the outer skin so an insect can grow.

nymph (NIMF) The young of an insect that looks like its adult form. Dragonfly young are nymphs.

paralyze (PER-uh-lyz) To stop prey from moving by poisoning it.

parasite (PER-uh-syt) An animal or plant that lives in or on another animal and is usually harmful to it.

predator (PREH-duh-ter) An animal that hunts and kills other animals (its prey) for food.

swarm (SWORM) A large number of insects, often in motion. The migratory phase of certain species.

victim (VIK-tim) A person or an animal that is harmed or killed.

Index

Web Sites

Due to the changing nature of Internet links, PowerKids Press has developed an online list of Web sites related to the subject of this book. This site is updated regularly. Please use this link to access the list: www.powerkidslinks.com/ask/bug/